Rhythmic Tests for Sight Reading

GRADE 8 TO ARCT

BY BORIS BERLIN
AND WARREN MOULD

Rhythmic Tests for Sight Reading

It is imperative, in order to successfully read a piece of music at sight, to take a moment to study the music before actually playing it in order to observe the phrase shape, the melodic outline, the harmonic structure, and to try to sense the overall rhythmic feeling of the music. Only then should you begin to play, striving to be as accurate as possible in notation and rhythm while, at the same time, taking care to observe the various interpretive indications provided, such as tempo markings, nuances of expression, pedalling, phrasing, and other directions which contribute to a musical performance of the piece.

Students who have not fully studied the Rhythmic Training Exercises and special Test material in the Workbooks of earlier grades are strongly advised to consult the "Basics of Ear Training" Teacher's Manual and Student Workbooks, Grades I to VII, published by Gordon V. Thompson, Limited.

This book, based on the Sight Reading requirements of the Royal Conservatory of Music and other major Examining Boards, has been prepared to provide students of advanced grades with exercises designed to assist them with the rhythmic portion of the Sight Reading Test of practical examinations. This specific test requires the candidate to clap at sight the rhythm of a given melody, which represents quite a different problem from that of clapping "blank" rhythms. The purpose of this is to assess the student's ability to recognize promptly and to understand not only melodic and harmonic formations but also rhythmic ones — a prerequisite for an accomplished sight-reader.

It should be borne in mind that in Sight Reading, rhythmic accuracy is at least as important, if not more so, than accuracy in notation. Therefore, the intensive study of rhythm and the resulting increased ability to perform more rhythmically will benefit the student by attaining a higher standard, not only in an examination, but also in the whole area of general performance proficiency. Thus he will be in a much more favourable position to truly "play for pleasure" as a result of his improved sight-reading ability. For this reason the student will be well advised not only to **clap** the exercises of this book, but also to **play** each exercise after clapping it.

Students should strive to clap correctly the exercise at first sight. Should this pose any particular difficulty, special Preparatory Exercises are provided on pages 16 to 24 of this Workbook. It is strongly urged that the student should not neglect these special exercises if **ANY** kind of difficulty is encountered.

In the event that a student finds even these Preliminary Exercises somewhat beyond his immediate capability it is recommended that he study the various development exercises provided in the earlier graded Workbooks of the "Basics of Ear Training" course, published by Gordon V. Thompson Limited.

Special Rhythmic Exercises at the Keyboard, based on more complex rhythms involving both hands simultaneously, will be found on page 19. On page 20 a number of excerpts are given from works of various well-known composers with examples of rhythmic problems found in piano compositions. These will, of course, not only assist the student in overcoming the rhythmic problems of these particular pieces but also help them to solve more easily many of the sight-reading problems encountered in the special tests at examinations.

Grade VIII

Clap or tap the rhythm of a melody in 3/4 or 6/8 time:
Frapper le rythme de la mélodie:

Grade VIII

Grade VIII

Grade IX

Clap or tap the rhythm of a melody in ¾ or 4/4 time:
Frapper le rythme de la mélodie:

Grade IX

Grade IX

Grade X

Clap or tap the rhythm of a melody in 2/4 or 3/4 time:
Frapper le rythme de la mélodie:

Grade X

Grade X

ARCT

Clap or tap the rhythm of a melody:
Frapper le rythme de la mélodie:

ARCT

ARCT

Preparatory Exercises

These exercises are designed to assist students in overcoming rhythmic problems of the more troublesome rhythmic units or patterns by understanding their structure.

In the following examples the <u>BASIC BEATS</u> (a) a ♩ in simple time and a ♩. in compound time, and their <u>subdivisions</u> (c) in ♪ illustrate the relative position in a bar of the notes comprising the rhythmic patterns (b).

It is recommended that these rhythms be practiced in the following manner: ① hum or say the rhythm to "*la, la*" while clapping or tapping the ♪ notes of the subdivision; and ② clap the rhythm while counting the basic beats.

Grade VIII

Grade IX

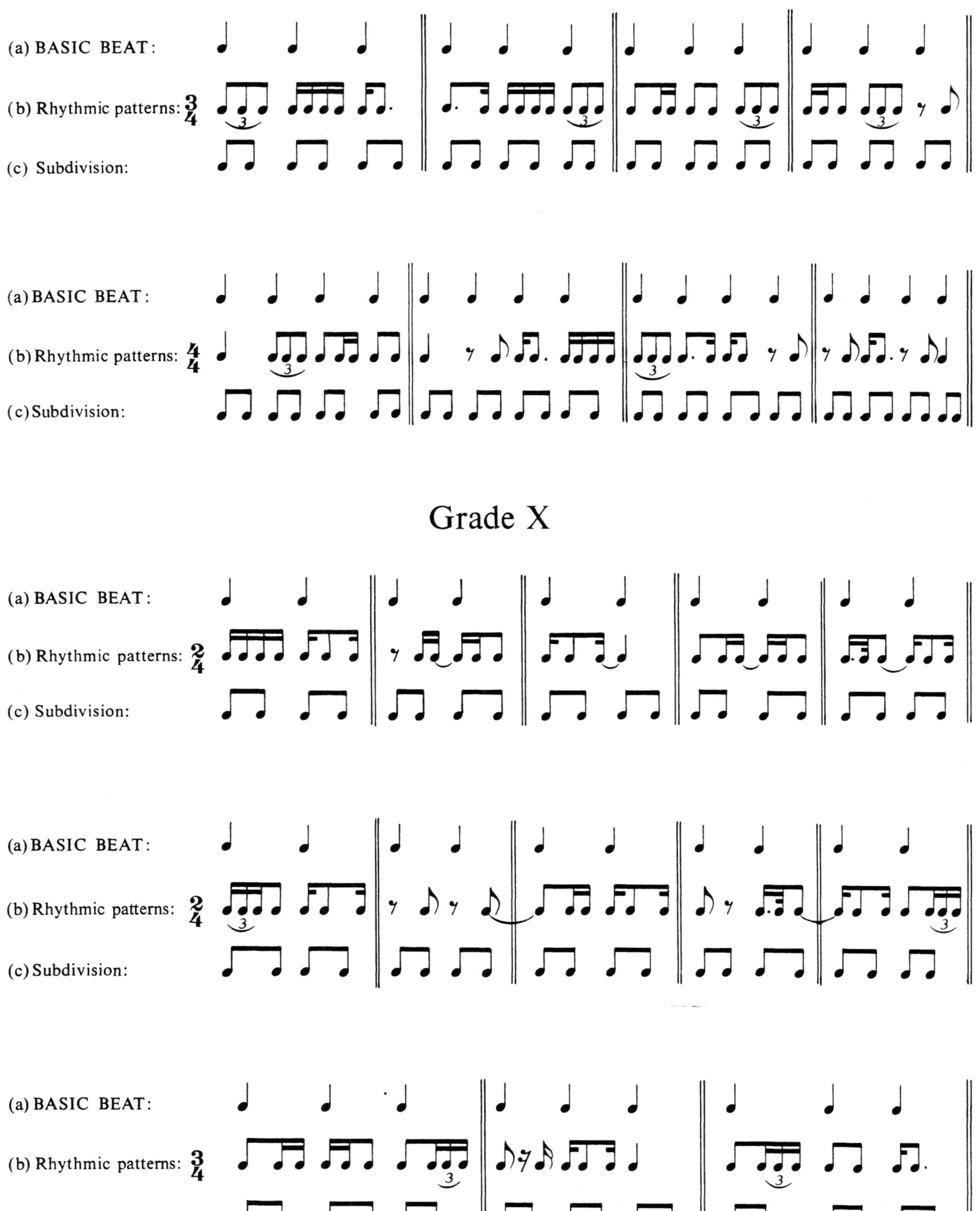

Grade X

ARCT

(a) BASIC BEAT

(b) Rhythmic patterns:

(c) Subdivision:

Rhythmic Exercises at the Keyboard

Various Rhythmic Problems Found in Piano Music
(polyrhythm, irregular time, changes in time-signatures, etc.)

Problem: grouping of 2+2+2+3 ♪ in 9/8 time.

Renée Sáint Jean

Problem: various subdivisions of a 𝅗𝅥 note beat 𝅗𝅥 = ♩ ♩ ‖ ♩ = ♫ = ♩♩♩ (3) ‖

DEBUSSY
(Hommage à Rameau)

Lent et grave
(dans le style d'une Sarabande mais sans rigueur)

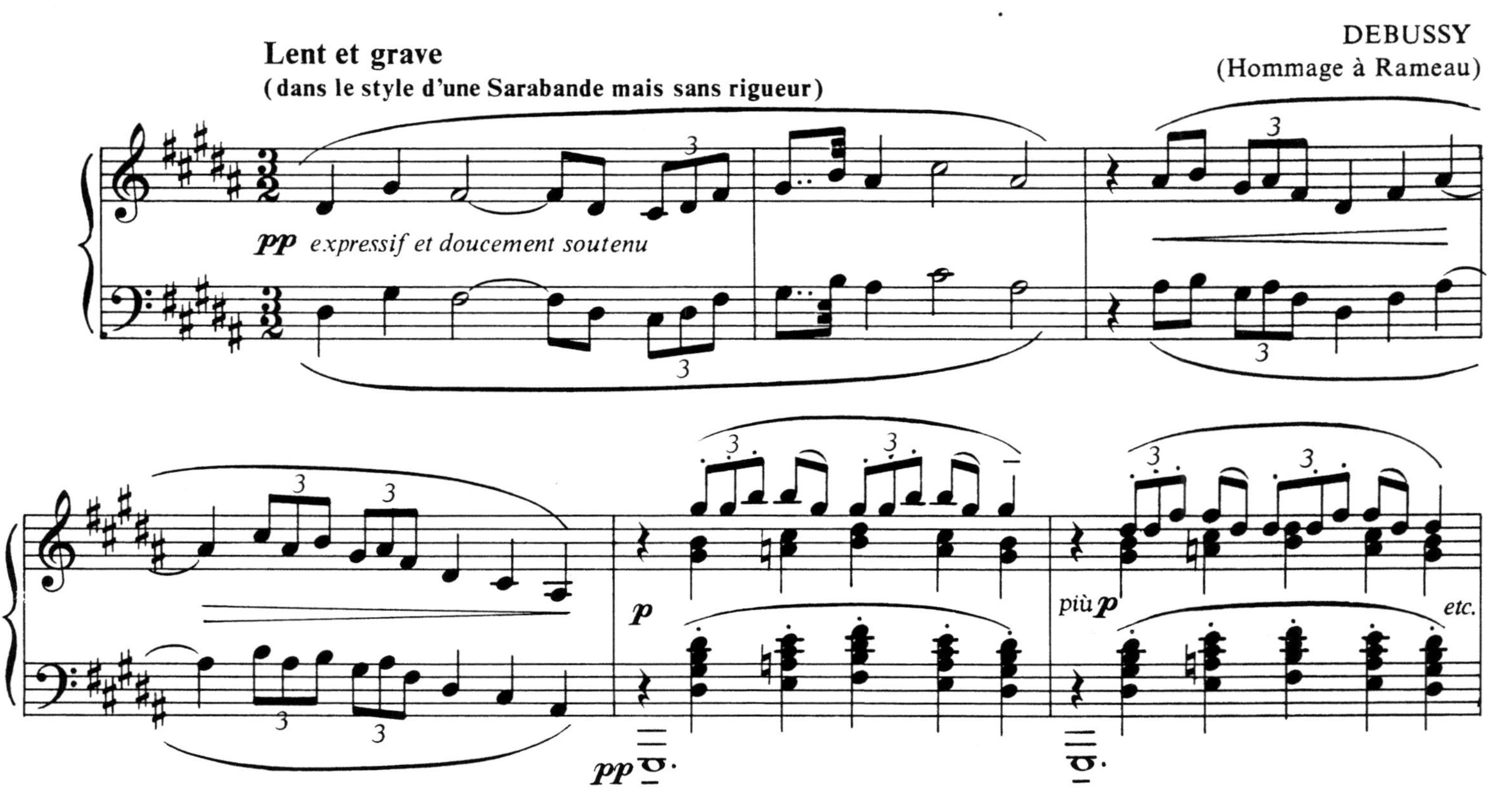

Problem: changes in time-signatures.

RENE SAINT JEAN

Andante ♪ = ♪

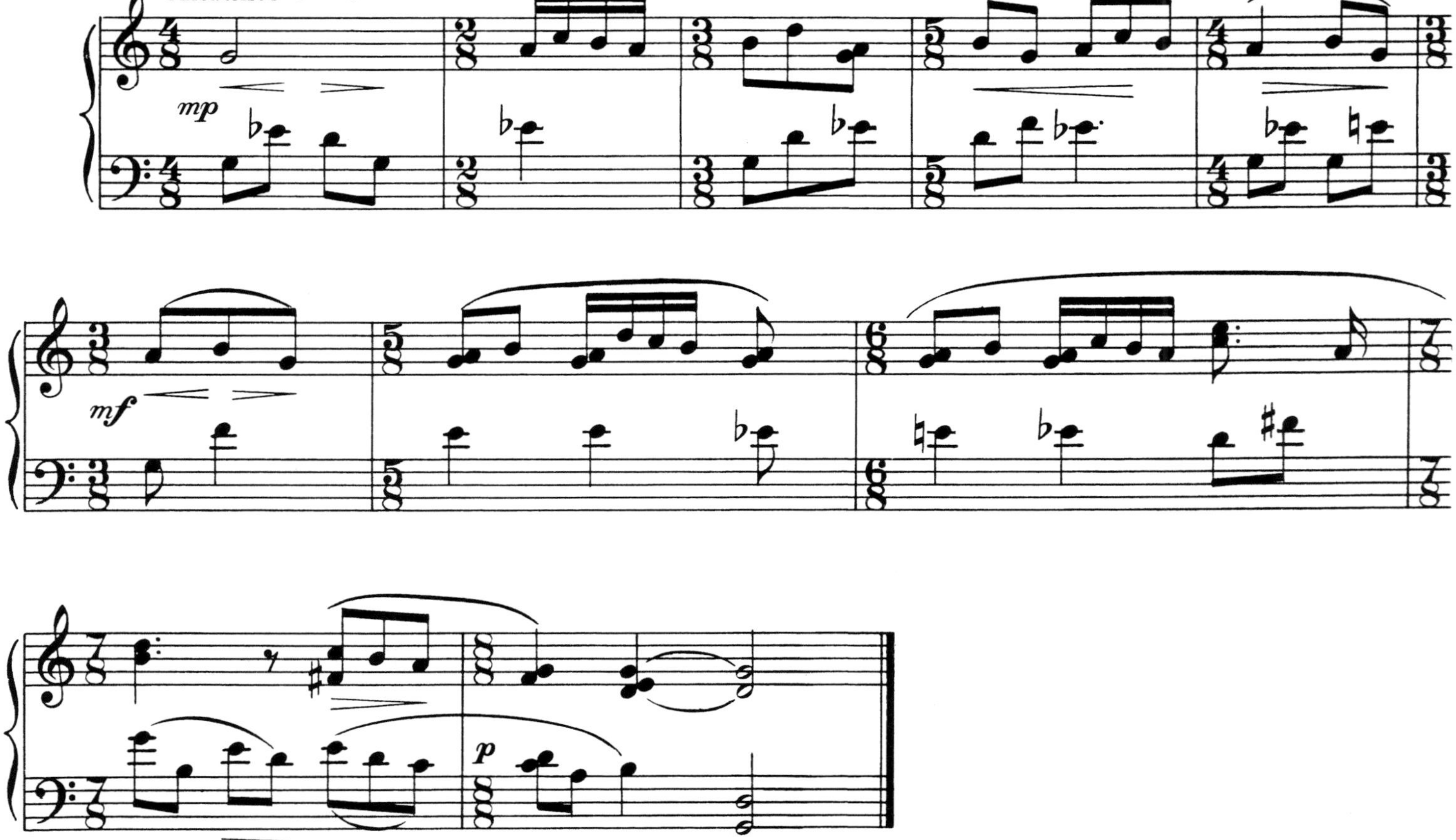

Problem: Polyrhythms:
BEETHOVEN
(Rondo Op 51 No 1)
Andante
p
sf
sf
Problem: 3 against 2.
CHOPIN (Etude)
Allegretto
sotto voce
una corda
Ped.
etc.

Problem: polyrhythm, 2 against 3, and 3 against 2

Problem: Duplets in compound time. $\dot{\quad}$

GRIEG (Nocturne)

Problem: Triplet quarter-notes against eighth notes. (4 against 3)

CHOPIN
(Etude in F minor)

Problems: various rhythmic groupings incorporated in a ♩ note basic beat;

WEBER Op. 40